ELEVATE YOUR ENERGY

E.Y.E

By: Damien R. Davis

Library of Congress Control Number   2019937863

ISBN: 978-0-578-48637-6   Softback

ISBN 9 7 8 -0-692-75395-8   E -Book

This book was printed in the United States America

To order additional copies of this book

Contact Amazon.com

www.rbpublishingin.com

barbara@rbpublishinginc.com

ACKNOWLEDGEMENTS

First and for most I would like to Thank God. My baby sister Rafinee for never to judged me I would like to also; I would like to thank my son Avery Ronnel KyAnte' and Zymeek my oldest.

I would like to thank my dad for helping me when I needed him the most. I would like to thank my big brother Alonzo.

Thank you Ms. Barbara Armstrong who is an amazing author and publisher Isiah Mullen who held me accountable through the process of finishing my book Last but not least I would like to thank the strongest woman I've ever known my mother

Rest in Peace R.I.P. Mrs. Yvonne R. Davis, I love you mama.

ELEVATE YOUR ENERGY

Introduction

E.Y.E

Is an eye opening easy read book for all walks of life this is a book I wrote during a time I was in a closed minded dark place. That influenced me to use my energy to level positive and negative boundaries which led me to write this inspiring self-elevation book which was all of the negative forces that kept me in this dark place and feeling down and out, I decided to find my own happiness through helping myself and others, it don't matter if it's just lying in a bed rubbing my two feet together, although it may sound dumb to some degree, there is people who are homeless with no bed to lie in. Before we rise to elevate we can't forget where we come from and losing sight of where we are going which is a common thing for most of us, regardless of your status education reputation, humans seek acceptance from one another should we uplift each other instead of bringing one another down. People need people to survive. No one want to die alone I know I don't is why I ask the world to elevate your energy.

YOUR ENERGY

The importance of your energy:

Your energy controls the outcome of your everyday living the people you influence and the people who influence your energy. Energy is found everywhere. We use energy when we sleep, sometime when we're not able to sleep it's because the thought is replaying in our head causing us to become drained, and when we become drained it's hard for us to stay motivated. Let's look at a definition for the word (energy) which means (in work) which is the capacity for doing work, because not all forms of energy can be converted into useful work it is more precise to say that the energy of a system changes by the amount equal to the net worth done on the system. Information can be found in the Grolier Encyclopedia of knowledge, with this being said I would like to challenge you to view your energy on a day to day basis, the first challenge involves you as the reader to pay attention to your normal reaction throughout your daily Interactions.

Challenge, notice the way you feel, when someone tell you (No).
Challenge pay attention to how you feel when someone tells you
(yes).
Challenge, I want you to make time for self. Make a time in the day when
you can close your eyes and meditate.

Challenge, I would like you to enter a room full of people.

Explanation: if you're wondering why I asked you to observe how it feel
when someone tells you no. The reason why most people are used to
hearing yes, always hearing yes can be a bad thing because hearing no
seems so foreign it might feel like rejection but rejection, is a normal part
of life plus what if you tell someone no wouldn't you want them to respect
your decision to say no without them putting out bad energy.
As agreed with you the feeling is good. But if you were right all the time
the error there would be no room for correction, people willing to learn is
willing to elevate their energy.

Explanation: Peace and quiet time. Here's a list of activities that may help you refocus your energy, try meditating, doing yoga, going out for a jog, relaxing in a quiet place to gather your thoughts or driving without a destination, these activities maybe therapeutic for the mind body and soul, many times in life we need a break from everything.

Explanation: after viewing how we interact, you should be able to read people body language and energy. Notice a room full of chaos and see where you fit in notice, now notice a room full of people that is quiet what's your first reaction to the crowd do you enter the room quiet would you disrupt the peace and quiet time? Whatever you decide is all up to you, but being able to read people energy is a gift not everyone can pick

ELEVATE YOUR ENERGY

WHAT'S AROUND YOU

Energy is everywhere it's inside of you, it come from the sun and we also get it from certain elements constantly fighting against the push and pulls of positive and negative forces of life which is another way to use our energy is to speak what the mind is thinking before our words can be manifested through our actions and mannerisms it's almost like reading a book by its cover just by looking at a book cover or its title you would think you could tell if it's interesting or not but the fact of the matter you may have to read the back of the book introduction to get into it just like getting to know someone you will have to be willing to accept that person for whom they are, but getting to know them is that whole new introduction that come over a time, new relationships can take energy and effort to evaluate the company you keep come with interaction and energy we get from each other is different from the energy we will get from our children and our pets. When our children see us foods such as: white sugars, brown sugar, honey proteins, starch which in turn provide us with proper diets and quick energy If you are looking have long lasting energy then you should eat more potatoes, rice, cereals, corn noodles bread sweet potatoes barley and pasta it's easy to maintain a healthy life style and promote energy inside of you. Well how about the desire to get anything done drives us to greater heights. What about when you had your first crush you would do anything to get that person to notice you it didn't matter how much energy it took you were determined to make that dream come true but after the desire is gone your energy level decrease in life they are so happy to see us, unlike our bosses or co- workers we work with on a day to day basis, children and pets don't judge us on our short comings, they accept us no matter what we've been through and we give them the same positive energy. What about that feeling you get from the sun? Does it bring back memories family vacations family reunions and trips to the lake? What a great thought for today

ELEVATE YOUR ENERGY

The balance of conversation while exercising your mind with good energy. A balanced conversation gives you a chance at talking and listening makes our energy positive.

Conversation is a balance between give or take if a conversation is boring it drains you causing negative energy.

The balance of fun time

The balance of conversation, or too much talking leads to less listening maybe a fruitless conversation negative energy, or learning new ways and opportunities and balance of fun time or having too much fun can lead to loss of drive i.e. negatives energy drugs alcohol missing work and extra curriculum activities balance of working our energy in the long run.

The balance of religion

It's so many religions to choose from but all have one thing in common and that is free will God never force us to believe in him no matter who invites us into his presence the choice is still ours to believe all we can be is a set example of God balance in all walk of our life to keep encouraging those around us to create good energy

The balance of groups
Working with others and getting along with others isn't mandatory However; being able to separate the positive and negative energy working with others mean a group of people who are using the same energy not balancing working habits become positive and negative forces

ELEVATE YOUR ENERGY

I invite you as the reader to take a journey with me the first part of this journey will require a TV with basic cable, now when you turn the TV on do you automatically have a certain show that you want to watch if that show is on do you settle for that show or through your curiosity run wild forcing you to search for something new the beauty of being able to change the channel is we can channel our energy the same way we change a channel this example shows us how we can re-channel our energy, and our thoughts our reality go hand in hand when going through our daily experiences depending on what gets stored go into our memory later in the day if that experience or interactions have deep impact on us it's more likely to weigh in on our mental , with that weighing in on us all day, we end up letting that thought ,or experience grow roots which cause us to use unnecessary energy that's needed to do something positive or creative remember we all have choices to choose from and our choice now is to elevate. What do you choose to do in life? To channel our energy that is stored inside of us let's say you're bored and there's nothing to do but you feel like something's missing in will believe it or not there probably is something that you can do with your energy. But you have to find out what that one thing it is, and that also require you to use energy putting that thinking into motion takes energy.

ELEVATE YOUR ENERGY

For us to channel into what we want to do for us to re-channel into what we're thinking I thought to myself, and I think a lot of us do in life, have you ever had to speak or read in front of a large group?

whenever I had to speak or read in front of a large group, right before I would usually, say to myself is just a way for me to calm my nerves and channel my energy actors use this technique a lot when you practice in front of a mirror you can be your own audience you become your own audience and it may get you prepared for a crowd so my suggestions for anyone stuck on one thought or channel it would be best to talk to yourself when you are more on a set channel that drains your energy.

ELEVATE YOUR ENERGY

REWIRING YOUR THINKING

What happens when you replace something over and over and over do you ever find a solution to the problem? Well we tend to go to sleep with it, and wake up to that same problem. We find it hard to believe that we would give a thought that never mattered so much Time & Energy and most of our thoughts usually end up being in someone else's problem but we are just human beings we don't possess special powers we can't read minds we can't be everywhere at once we can change the way we think all we can do as friends fathers, mothers, daughters, sisters, husbands and wives is change the way we think and change the way we treat one another. In this new day and age it's a bigger monster influencing the way we think and interact called, the internet / social media now the internet do have those have these pros and cons and a good thing about the online hype is fast and easy access to music dating the website and on line shopping sites, but the downfall to this popular addicting phenomenal is the lack of privacy and after something of you has been posted online you cannot protect yourself. The question has been raised more and more over the past couple of years and the question has been about purposely leak sex tapes now the average person would lose their mind to something so personal, but super stars has found a way and overcome the unthinkable turning something that's looked upon as negative into something they feel inspiring There's more than one way to feel confident about something. Read while you are thinking means to change the way you would normally think using cognitive thinking is key you've heard many say write down any of your dream goals and invention the reason is having a visual of something written in words is another way to bring your thoughts into existence what if you forgot about an idea that you came up with if you would have written it down it would have made it that much easier to remember In this book it would be best to remember the chapter to keep it locked into your brain many times we've read and learn something and somewhere down the line we forget what we thought we have learned, using your brain is a process there's many ways to think and feel, so don't get caught up in feeling like their way is the only way.

ELEVATE YOUR ENERGY

HIGH ENERGY SCORE

What's so important about getting a high energy score for start, having a higher score on any test, should give you a good feeling. Scoring my energy was never brought to my attention, so I came up with an energy questioner it's a ten Yes or No test that determine if you have a positive or negative energy . It may or may not show you how you're securitized by the world and how the world looks at you. Do you believe leaving a legacy important to you? Believe it or not we're always watched and judged for our actions. When people look at you what are they seeing? Happiness sadness, anger, lost, determined, fearful, courageous all of these expressions can be seen by others a developing mind is an important aspect of emotions and social function. Emotions both primary and categorical serve as the vehicles that allow one person to have a sense of the mental state of another. The capacity to feel another person has many labels such compassion, empathy, sympathy, mirroring, or mind sight. In its essence the ability of one mind to perceive and experience elements of a person's mind is profoundly important dimension of human experience. I agree with the statement in full because we all feed off each other so after learning that I want you to know that getting a high energy score won't instantly solve all of your problems, but getting a higher score will open your eyes to your energy. The cool thing about a low score is working toward getting a higher energy score. It's all on you.

ELEVATE YOUR ENERGY

POSITIVE ENERGY SCORE

On a scale from one to ten, how would you rate yourself say all around you are about a five, six or maybe a seven. Having a positive energy important in our daily life interactions well I'll tell you why I think having a positive energy score can help ask yourself a few questions can you maintain regular conversations, keep a steady relationship, or feel comfortable speaking at a job interview are in public ? A positive energy score were made to give you a better result in life after scoring your energy let's see you get as close to 10 are 100% as possible. How to operate your energy score it's easy first answer both positive and negative questions and the more plus signs you have the closer you are to having a 100 percent.

Example if you have 17 plus signs out of 20 questions then multiply the 17 plus signs by 100 then divide the 1700 by 20 questions which will leave you with 85 percent. Also if none of the questions apply to you I challenge you to make your own negative and positive questions.

Do you think and speak positively

If no then the chances of you speaking positive are slim to none, if we are always thinking negative your more than likely speaking the same way you're feeling. if we are speaking positive while going through a life crisis when your energy level is positive your expression will likely show our energy level you will speak it positive energy into existence of people who maybe suffering from disease or chance to work on your positive energy, the less negative score the better your positive energy score.

Grading your negative energy score has the same process, except you want to get the lowest score possible Example: add all the negative signs multiply the amount by 100 then by 11 by 10

If yes, then it's time for you to focus on self because you are allowing others to control your energy it's up to you and what you allow that affect your life.

Do you use manipulation as a tool?

If yes using manipulation to influence others can cause major damage to you or others around you which can consume your positive energy. Be aware of malicious ways that can harm you and those closest to you protected.
  If no manipulation is being used beware that influencing and manipulation to control people all go hand in hand each take both positive energy and negative energy depending on how it is used.

DO you thrive on violence?

The pros and cons of violence have its advantage and disadvantages which you consider carefully so that you can make sensible decisions when you are angered. Control your emotions which contribute to your energy violence is a form of anger which consumes your energy. Anger is a primary emotion wired to our energy system when boundaries are crossed use meditation as a way to control anger.

Are you vengeful what if you waste many years waiting on payback and let's say you finally do and you're not satisfied how much energy you have wasted

ELEVATE YOUR ENERGY

NEGATIVE ENERGY SCORE

Are you vulnerable if yes what if you waste so many years waiting on Revenge and let's say you finally get revenge and it doesn't satisfy how much energy you wasted. If no then you have learnt how that you don't have explain or prove anything to anyone the only person you owe is you.

Do you get the proper amount of sleep?

Yes then you're prepared for what's to come in your day. We always heard the body needs 8 hours to regurgitate when the body has exhausted all energy it could take 6-7 hours lack of sleep may cause you to be sluggish throughout the day you may come off as irritable you may trying to find sleep while on the job or at school.

Have you ever considered getting professional help?

Yes then you are willing to start the healing process, we all need to find out what's going on inside of us. If no then you don't know what you could be holding on to being able to talk to someone who's willing to listen and not judge can prevent someone falling into depression or prevent someone from committing suicide.

Are you a sore loser?

We can't win in life if we don't go through the up and downs every time you feel like you're winning you are actually becoming better at falling hard when you do lose. When you lose you know you'll have an opportunity to win again

Are you in denial no you will not hold yourself accountable for your actions or responsibilities.

Yes then you're not in denial and you can admit when you are wrong you also can feel empathy for those who have dealt with the same problems in life making it easier to relate to every human being.

ELEVATE YOUR ENERGY

ALL YOU EVER NEVER NEEDED WAS YOU

Who am I? Why am I here? I ask myself these questions constantly saying we know ourselves completely would be a bold face lie, because we learn new things about ourselves everyday certain foods I used to I used to dislike when I was a child now that I've grown to like such as green peas but if I never gave those peas a chance and learned that I just had to dress them in a way to fit my taste buds I probably would have never learned that I actually like pea salad. It all boils down to how it works for us. See in life everyone won't have the same likes or dislikes, some people may never like or believe in us and that's okay because I believe in me as you should too. Some people cross your life with different opinions of you is always against you it's best to keep those negative energy away from your daily routine remember likeminded people wants to see you win the positive energy they bring such as : stability, success, happiness all of those goals and anything that's positive should feel good. For some it's hard to identify with their feelings because were all constantly changing.

I remember when I was young there was popular movie at the time called The Last Dragon the main character was Bruce Leroy throughout the movie he searched to find this great martial artist who never existed because the master was already inside of Bruce Leroy. Sometime we try to find in others what we already possess it's just not time to be revealed to us it's just give it time don't forceit.

ELEVATE YOUR ENERGY

LOSING FOCUS

I lost focus while I was writing my energy was off because of negative thoughts going through my mind until I told myself it's time to regain focus so I can elevate my energy. There are so many ways to get side tracked when you pose low energy another problem with losing focus When your energy slow the entire negative outside forces fighting to Take your eyes off the prize we should always be the prize it's in light making a hundred plans and never completing one of them what are You focused on is it the very thing that doesn't matter well it's the same energy that clouds your brain is also affecting your energy. Yet focusing on something positive should help you physically and mentally that's why it's important to distinguish what you focusing on staying

Elevated means staying focus on something that's above all distractions, not thinking you are above everyone but only focusing on your energy

it's the possession part of elevating your energy that you mainly need to focus on if you focus on elevating your energy then you don't have to worry about the crabs in a bucket theory one waiting to pull the other crab down once it reaches the top instead of latching on to the one that reaches the top to form a chain for everyone to climb out of the bucket.

ELEVATE YOUR ENERGY

Regaining Complete Awareness

Unfortunately it's pretty much impossible to have complete awareness at all times but being able to be aware at all make a big difference in the book the seven habits of high effective people the author Stephan Kory speaks about the goose and the golden egg. The story is about a poor farmer who discovers in the nest of his pet goose a glittering golden egg. At first he think it's some kind of trick but as he starts to throw the egg aside he has a second thought and takes it in to be appraised instead the egg is pure gold the farmer can't believe his fortune he becomes even more incredulous the following day he awakens to the nest and finds another golden egg he becomes fabulous wealthy it all seems too good to be true with his increasing wealth come greed and Impatience unable to wait day after day after day for the golden eggs the farmer decides to kill the goose and get then all at one once but when he opens the goose he finds it empty there are no golden eggs and now there's no way to get anymore eggs the farmer has destroyed the goose that produced them, the author this explains that his fable pertained to natural law a principle definition of effectiveness lies imbalance.

ELEVATE YOUR ENERGY

Regaining Complete Awareness

Continues Elevate your energy shares the same principles by balancing your energy now had the farmer been aware that he could become greedy if the opportunity presented itself rushing to get more golden eggs would have been the last thing on his mind yet in life we are not always aware of how we would react to every situation that is thrown at us. I would advise everyone to be aware of self because when you are aware of what you are doing you are fully responsible of your actions being aware gives you the advantage of what you are learning and what you're not learning for instance when you're at school or at work when it's time to show your work you will be put to the test and that's why it's important to constantly stay working on self. Let's say you're in school to become a barber and you are not sure of a haircut you've just done if you are not sure you are not completely aware of what you're doing that haircut is vital to your grade that client and your pride In certain professions where complete awareness is so important Here's a list of professions where complete awareness is severely important open heart surgeons airline pilots live band performers NASCAR drivers UFC fighters professional sport players day to day drivers automobiles and people in charge of heavy machine equipment mothers and fathers and the list go on gaining awareness is easier said than done all you have to do is be aware that you are not aware of being aware which is basically means pay attention to what's going with your thoughts and energy.

About the author:

Damien Davis grew up in the streets of Tacoma WA. Where he gained most of his skills and swagger He later moved down south and although the East coast and the West coast he got to see the world from many different angles. One of those angles being the rough streets of Baltimore MD. To brushing shoulders with scholars and professors at the university of Washington but dealing with life without a father figure Damien hit a couple of road blocks but he was still able to elevate his energy and find happiness.

ELEVATE YOUR ENERY

Positive Encouragement Strength Determination Love

Negative energy

Chronically thinking cause depression anxiety disorders,
Distorted by fear of the unknown it is disturbing for a person to realize everything in life rather in our control or out of our control. It can come from anxious doubtful which is a lack of faith if we speak in biblical terms let's look at the overall of positive energy.

Positive Energy

Thinking well we can confidently say depression is gone with the proper help and prayer. Anxiety is replaced with be anxious for nothing that we cannot change or control. Fear is change with confidence and doubt authority most of all positivity and love.

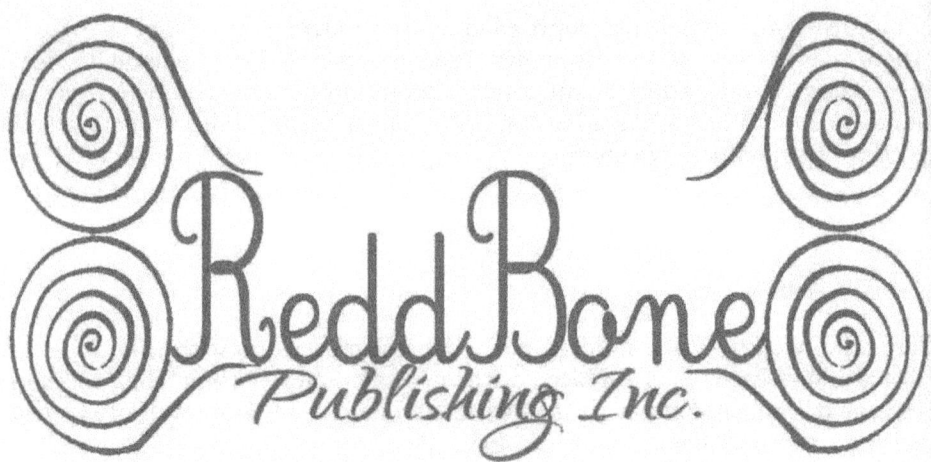

PUBLISHED BY: REDDBONE PUBLISHING INC. @ 2017